*To*

_____

*From*

_____

*Date*

_____

*"Greatness is in You* is well-written and easy to follow. The section on goals, in itself, is worth the price of admission! As a wise man once said, we go to school to learn a lot of things. Yet, one of the key indicators of success in life – the ability to set and accomplish goals - is never taught in schools!

My prayer is that every reader will take action on the points Opeyemi has outlined in this book.

Be blessed as you read."

**—Tunji Osinulu**
Houston, TX


*"Greatness is in You* is a must read for anyone looking to live out their passion and fulfill their destiny. Loaded with insightful and expository truths from the word of God, this is an excellent resource for those seeking to "take the bull by the horn" and maximize their full potential."

**—Motolani Abike,**
Pastor @ The Well, and founder of Master's Mind Network.

"Wow! Wisdom for the season. Timely. Inspirational. Impactful. Transformational!"

**—Pastor Ayo Ajayi,**
RCCG, Salvation Center, Katy, TX

"Fervent. Passionate. Stirring. In Greatness Is In You, Ope challenges you to rise above limitations that defy your God-given potential. This book will get you thinking, stir you in the right direction, and leave you ignited, so you'll finally rise up to your life."

**—Jokotade**
International Artist, Multi-Creative
Entrepreneur, Speaker

"This is a must read for anyone ready to move to the next level. This book takes us through a powerful journey of self discovery. It's like a compass for a sailor lost in the deep sea and furiously maneuvering for the shore. There are golden spiritual nuggets spread throughout this book and I highly recommend it to everyone wanting to rise from the ashes of perennial struggles to live to their fullest potentials."

**—Ass. Pastor Sola Adegoke**
RCCG, Salvation Center, Katy, TX

# GREATNESS
## IS IN YOU

10 Essential Principles for Achieving Greatness

THE
CORNERSTONE
PUBLISHING

OPE ADEBAYO

**Published by:**
Cornerstone Publishing
A Division of Cornerstone Creativity Group LLC
Info@thecornerstonepublishers.com
www.thecornerstonepublishers.com
516.547.4999

**Author's Contact**

For booking to speak at your next event or to order bulk copies of this book please use information below:

+1 (346) 404 3212  |  info@opeadebayo.com

wwww.opeadebayo.com

# CONTENTS

# DEDICATION

To the Almighty GOD, my creator, strong pillar, source of inspiration, wisdom, knowledge and understanding, and the reason for my being.

# ACKNOWLEDGMENTS

Very special thanks to my darling husband, Adewale, for his constant love, and for not just believing, but knowing that I could do this! I love you always and forever!

To my wonderful son, David, you inspire me every time. Mommy loves you more than you will ever know.

Words alone cannot express my gratitude to Pastors Ayodeji and Layide Ajayi, Pastor Tunji Osinulu, Pastor Tolani Akingbade, Pastor Shola Adegoke, and Mrs Jokotade, for their great contributions, timely support, words of encouragements, and prayers. You are highly appreciated.

Many thanks to Pastor Gbenga Showunmi and his team at Cornerstone Publishing, for the preparation of this manuscript, for the timely support, and for keeping me on track every time. Thank you for making this happen.

My acknowledgements would be incomplete

without thanking my biggest source of strength, "my family". To my late father, thank you for the virtues of greatness instilled in me. You were the epitome of a great father and I couldn't have asked for a better one. Thank you, Dad, for everything. I miss and love you so much!

To my loving mother, the strongest woman I have ever known - a great source of inspiration and an incredible role model to me - thank you for your prayers and blessings! You are the best; I love you mum! To my loving siblings, without you, my entire world is empty. Thank you for being there every time. You all are amazing!

My appreciation also goes to all my friends for their assistance in bringing this vision to reality. God bless you all.

# INTRODUCTION

The journey of a thousand miles does not only begin with the first step, it begins with the first step of faith. Faith takes you into the hidden land of greatness—and the path of every great life requires navigating this land. As Hebrews 11:2 says, it was by taking this extraordinary step that the "elders" (pioneers of greatness) obtained a good report. That was the secret of their success – choosing to see, believe and declare the invisible, despite the many negative sights and sounds around them.

If you think that greatness is not for you, think again. You serve a good God who has predestined you to be the head and not the tail; to be above only and not beneath. You serve a great God who has mapped out great plans for your life. And you serve a mighty God who's able to turn your weaknesses to strengths and make the best out of the worst experiences of your life.

So, then, whatever you currently think you are capable of achieving, begin to think bigger because you can actually do much more! Never settle for a "this-is-good-enough" mentality - because once you do, you will live an average, mediocre life; a life that lacks glow. God's desire and expectation of you is that you continue to explore and excel. Reason? Because you've got all it takes to achieve the incredible.

Now is the time to shake off the fetters of negative assumptions and wake up to the certainties of your exalted position as a beloved child of God. Know for sure that mediocrity is not in your genes. You have greatness planted in your DNA. The anointing for excellence flows in your veins, and the power to conquer obstacles and limitations lies within you - if only you will stir it up.

A life of greatness will require you to grab the ball and run with it. It requires that you get rid of wishful thinking and start taking decisive steps towards the fulfillment of your aspirations. Get some thick skin in the game. Put feet to your dreams. Your future is filled with unlimited opportunities; so go for it! You are all wired for greatness! You were born for this!

# ONE

## IT BEGINS WITH YOUR MIND

*"Guard your heart above all else, for it determines the course of your life" (Proverbs 4:23, NLT).*

---

Everything in life begins from the mind. This includes success and greatness. Before every physical manifestation of success and excellence, the mind must have been habitually tuned, pruned and groomed towards it. The implication of this is that your thoughts create and shape who you truly are.

Your mind is the driving force of your life. It is the seedbed from which the circumstances that surround you grow. I can personally confirm this because, several times, I have allowed my mind to get the better of me, resulting in different noticeable outcomes – depending on the kind of power I allow it to wield upon me.

This is why God, who placed the engine of the mind within us, strictly counsels, "Guard your heart above all else, for it determines the course of your life" (Proverbs 4:23, NLT). The King James Version puts it this way, "Keep thy heart with all diligence; for out of it are the issues of life." Both of these translations are saying the same thing, in different but meaningful ways. While one speaks of the power of the mind on the individual, the other reveals its influence on life in general – and both are certainly true.

In the general sense of it, look all around you, and you will realize why the mind is rightly described as the fountain, wellspring or seedbed of the issues of life. See if you can find anything in the world that did not originate from the mind. To begin with, the entire universe itself originated from the mind of God. God conceived the idea of everything He wanted to see before calling it forth. This is why He found everything to be "good" because each manifested according to His expectation.

Good enough for you and for me, we have been placed on earth to be God's representatives, which was why He had to personally breathe into us. In other words, we have received the divine impartation (or you may call it the divine empowerment) to continue to unleash the power of creativity upon the earth – and of course, upon our own very lives!

So, I ask you again, look around to see if there is any useful product or structure which you can say appeared on its own. Think about the awesome masterpieces of art, the mind-blowing discoveries of science, the wondrous possibilities of technology and the jaw-dropping constructions of engineering. Think of powerful empires and dynasties. Think of the many successful and multibillion dollar companies and corporations all around. Think of world-changing ideas, speeches, inventions, revolutions, revivals and breakthroughs. They all began with that powerhouse within us called the mind. Somebody somewhere began the imagination that ultimately resulted in each of these realities that have continued to inspire, impress and challenge us.

Sadly, the same is true of the diverse evils, crises, conflicts and bloodshed that we witness daily. The processes that are involved, as well as the forces that combine to bring these evils to manifestation, are always triggered by the imagination of someone. Maybe you can now understand why God tells us to guard our minds.

Note it again – in the mind is where it all begins! Success and failure begin from the mind. Possibilities and limitations begin from the mind.

Courage and fear begin from the mind. Excellence and mediocrity begin from the mind. Peace and conflicts begin from the mind…and the list goes on and on.

# THE PERSONAL ANGLE

The general application aside, what all this means for you is that you have within you, what you can use to direct the course of your life to a desirable destination. You have within you what you can use to build or rebuild your life and make your future enviable. It also means that if you do not construct success within you, you cannot have its manifestation in your life. Above all, it means that as long as you are not defeated in your mind, you can never be defeated in the physical; as long as you do not conclude that you are a failure in your mind, you can never become a failure in life.

So, friend, know that the decision is ultimately yours to conceive and construct the life you wish to have in your mind. It is the spiritual that controls the physical, and not the other way around. As the Scripture says, "For as he thinks in his heart, so is he…" (Proverbs 23:7). Your life brings into reality what your mind constantly feeds your subconscious.

# DECIDING YOUR FUTURE, REGARDLESS OF YOUR PAST

Your mind holds the key to unlocking an incredible future, irrespective of how horrible your past may have been. God Himself has given you the assurance, saying, *"Do not remember the former things, nor consider the things of old. Behold, I will do a new thing…" (Isaiah 43:18-19).*

What this means is that your past does not necessarily have the power to determine your future. How often do we hear people blame their present conditions on poor or dysfunctional family background, lack of support, abuse, financial challenges, or even racial or gender discrimination? Yet, none of this is the actual cause of their underachievement. While I am not discounting or minimizing the reality of their past situation, the real culprit stealing their present joy is the state of their mind.

So, it's time to quit blaming people or circumstances and tackle the real source of our limitations. How do we do this? The Bible provides the answer! "Be not conformed…but be ye transformed by the renewing of your mind" (Romans 12:2).

The secret of living a life of peace, joy, impact, achievement and fulfillment lies in choosing to be transformed, rather than conforming to the limitations of your past and the expectations of your critics. And how do you do this? By RENEWING your mind – in other words, changing your mindset!

Know it for sure now that instead of conforming to external limitations or your personal weaknesses, you can transform your life and destiny if you can look away from everything else and focus on your mind. Forget what everyone else has said or is saying – what is YOUR mind saying? This is the core of the matter.

## TRAINING YOUR MIND FOR GREATNESS

Now that you know that you carry the power of greatness within you through your mind, it is time to begin to take steps towards renewing and guarding it, as the Scripture has counseled.

You renew your mind by feeding it with positive nourishments. Philippians 4:6 (AMP) tells us what these nourishments are: "Finally, believers, whatever is true, whatever is honorable and worthy of respect, whatever is right and confirmed by God's word, whatever is pure and wholesome, whatever is lovely and brings peace, whatever is admirable and of good repute; if there is any excellence, if there is anything worthy of praise, think continually on these things [center your mind on them, and implant them in your heart]."

Feed your mind daily with what is true – what God is saying about you, not what people, your environment or natural senses are saying. What is God saying? That you are fearfully and wonderfully made; that you are destined to be the head and not the tail; that you can do all things through Christ who gives you strength; that He will supply all your needs according to His riches in glory; that you are beloved and blessed, not worthless or forsaken.

Again, it says to feed your mind with only pure and wholesome information – information that is uplifting and edifying. Read books, watch movies and listen to people that inspire you towards greatness; that help you to discover your inner strengths, develop courage to overcome obstacles and generally become a better YOU.

And then it says to think of excellence, not limitations or negative circumstances.

## SAFEGUARDING YOUR MIND

Just as there are things to nourish your mind with, so are there destroyers that must be kept far away from it. What this means is that there are several forces that are always seeking residence in your mind to influence its operation. These include joy, peace, success and positivity on the one hand; as well as negativity, fear, low self-esteem, depression and anxiety on the other. The question is, which of these are you giving room in your mind? What is your choice?

As for me, you can bet, I'm committed to choosing success, peace, positivity, joy and other boosters of the mind. Has it been easy? Nope! Has it been worth it? Oh yes!

I urge you to keep away the forces of negativity from your mind. As much as possible, avoid information, people, reports and places that can poison your mind, kill your joy, deflate your self-esteem or magnify your weaknesses.

Most importantly, there is a particular lousy friend that can prove really harmful to your dreams and decisions. It is called FEAR! Fear itself is as fearful as it sounds. It has been rightly described as False Evidence Appearing Real! Fear is a thought that something unpleasant may happen or may have happened. Fear is powerful, and many people (including myself), have been victims and, many more are still victims today.

The reality is that whether you are a victor over fear or a victim of it will depend on the kinds of thoughts you allow to dominate your mind. So, let me ask you: What thoughts are you feeding your mind? Positive thoughts or negative ones? To conquer fear, you must feed your mind right at all times. Refuse to be pushed around by fear; rather, choose to be led by the light of God's word in your heart.

There was a time in my life that I used to allow fear to limit me. I had all kinds of fears - fear of the unknown, fear of not being accepted, fear of failure, fear of taking decisions, fear of criticisms, fear of not being the best, fear of voicing out…it was fear all the way. Of course, because of this, I got stuck in a position where, for a long time. I was practically crippled. I couldn't achieve much!

However, one fateful day, I got fed up of my situation, and I cried – really cried - and prayed to God! And He reminded me of His promise in Isaiah 43:1, "…Fear not, for I have redeemed you; I have called you by your name; You are Mine." He also brought to mind His assurance in Deuteronomy 31:8, "And the Lord, He is the One who goes before you. He will be with you, He will not leave you nor forsake you; do not fear nor be dismayed." That was the end of the dominion of fear in my life.

# OVERCOMING FEAR

God knows that the devil can easily use fear to torment and cripple us by planting evil thoughts in our minds. That is why He informs us in Ephesians 6:12, that "we do not wrestle against flesh and blood, but against principalities, against powers, against the rulers of the darkness of this age, against spiritual hosts of wickedness in the heavenly places." But, praise God, we have the ultimate weapon against fear and that is the Word of God. Moreover, the Scripture tells us that "For God has not given us a spirit of fear, but of power and of love and of a sound mind" (2 Timothy 1:7).

You overcome fear by first believing in the word of God and in His power that is at work in your life. Face your fears daily by studying and meditating on God's words. Key into His words and know for sure that whatsoever challenge you are experiencing now is just a phase and it will pass away.

There once was this criminal who had committed a crime. (Because, hey, that's what criminals do. That's their job!). Anyway, he was sent to the king for his punishment.The king told him he had a choice of two punishments. He could be hung by a rope. Or take what's behind the big, dark, scary, iron door.

The criminal quickly decided on the rope. As the noose was being slipped on him, he turned to the king and asked: "By the way, out of curiosity, what's behind that door?"

The king laughed and said: "You know, it's funny, I offer everyone the same choice, and nearly everyone picks the rope."

"So," said the criminal, "Tell me. What's behind the door? I mean, obviously, I won't tell anyone," he said, pointing to the noose around his neck. The king paused then answered: "Freedom, but it seems most people are so afraid of the unknown that they immediately take the rope."

What happens when you overcome fear?

You enjoy happiness, refreshed mind, divine peace, focus, inspirations, ideas, confidence, productivity, inner and outer beauty, as well as attracting great things your life.

*Marianne Williamson* said, "Our deepest fear is not that we are inadequate. Our deepest fear in that we are powerful beyond measure. It is our Light, not our Darkness, that most frightens us.

We ask ourselves, who am I to be brilliant, gorgeous, talented, fabulous? Actually, who are you not to be? You are a child of God. Your playing small does not serve the World.

There is nothing enlightening about shrinking so that other people won't feel unsure around you. We were born to make manifest the glory of God that is within us. It is not just in some of us; it is in everyone. As we let our own Light shine, we consciously give other people permission to do the same.

As we are liberated from our own fear, our presence automatically liberates others."

Let me remind you again: To be great in life, it starts from your mind, whatsoever positive things your mind can conceive, you can achieve. Believe you can do it, set your mind to it and you will ACHIEVE it!

# TWO

## POWER OF SELF-AWARENESS

*"I will praise You, for I am fearfully and wonderfully made; Marvelous are Your works, And that my soul knows very well." (Psalm 139:14)*

---

One of the notable characteristics you will find in all great achievers in life is that they have a good knowledge of themselves and appreciate their uniqueness. They don't try to be someone else or live their lives according to people's opinions or trending lifestyles. Their happiness is not dependent on the approval and affirmations of others. Or to apply it to our current social media world, their happiness does not depend on how many followers they have or how many "likes" they get; nor is their beauty dependent on how much they conform to a celebrity's beauty regimen.

These people, like David the Psalmist, believe that they have been fearfully and wonderfully made and, therefore, need not make themselves a photocopy of someone else.

## SELF-APPLICATION

So, let's come to you, friend. What do you think of yourself? Do you see yourself as being uniquely made, loaded with potentials and with a distinct assignment on earth, or do you see yourself as just an attachment, who is meant to dance to the tune of all else? Are you convinced that the fact that no one else, out the billions of people in the world, has the same fingerprint or DNA like yours, means that God specially crafted you and wants you to live YOUR own life in a distinct way?

This is important because your perception of yourself will not only affect the way you live your life but also the way people end up treating you. You have to love and accept yourself, flaws and all, in order for you to love and accept another person, flaws and all. If you don't get to know yourself, and learn how to love and accept yourself how will you get to know someone else and love and accept them? You can't have one without the other.

As for me, I have to admit that I used to see myself

as a nonentity. Thank God, however, that my eyes soon got opened and I came to understand who I am in Christ. I have come to realize that I, Oluwakemi, am fearfully and wonderfully made! I can do all things through Christ who gives me strength. I am destined for greatness. I am blessed, strong and highly favored. I walk in grace and live in grace. I see myself as a woman who is strong-willed, passionate about my goals, determined, driven, focused, creative, happy, confident, bold and so forth.

Again, let me ask you - who do you think you are? How do you see yourself? It's not about what everyone else thinks or says about you. It is about what you know yourself to be, especially if you have become a member of the family of God. See, becoming a child of God goes beyond merely forsaking your old life and making Christ your Savior. It actually transforms your being and gives you a brand new identity. 2 Corinthians 5:17-18 says, "Therefore, if anyone is in Christ, he is a new creation; old things have passed away; behold, all things have become new. Now all things are of God..."

Come on, did you see THAT? "Now all things are of God". So, what matters at this moment is not the filthiness of your past or the visible challenges of your present life. Rather, what matters is how God sees you and what God is saying about you. How does God see you? Don't search too far. Here it is: "But you are a chosen generation, a royal priesthood, a holy nation, His own special people, that you may proclaim the praises of Him who called you out of darkness into His marvelous light" (2 Peter 2:9).

What else do you need, friend? The Creator of heaven and earth says you are CHOSEN. He says you are SPECIAL – meaning that you are not just like any other person. It means that you are EXTRAORDINARY, with uncommon privileges and abilities! Why then are you still bothered about people's gossip and criticisms? Why then do you still consider yourself ugly or inferior? Why do you see yourself as limited, handicapped or disadvantaged? Come off it – you are far above that level!

Again, let me show you what God is saying about you.

He says you are:

1. **Salt and light of the world** (Matthew 5:13-14, Philippians 2:15). This means that you carry the message and power of hope within you. It means that without you, the world is hopeless. You have within you the key to open the prison doors of many who are bound in addictions

and afflictions. You have the power of liberty and breakthrough within you. Through you, sadness and depression should give way to gladness and joy. Through you, the hopeless should find hope and the helpless should find redemption.

2. **Child of light** (1 Thessalonians 5:5). This means that you carry within you the power to banish darkness in all its forms and manifestations. It means that you have the authority to confront and conquer the works and workers of darkness. It means that wherever you are, darkness, ignorance, affliction, oppression, depression and confusion cannot remain. All must give way because you are an uncommon being.

3. **Carrier of God's glory** (Isaiah 60:1-3). This means that wherever you go, you carry the glory of God with you and therefore you MUST be noticed. And you must be favored. There cannot be any reproach in your life because the glory of God overshadows your weaknesses. This glory makes you a natural champion. It makes you immune to defeat and disgrace. It makes you the head and not the tail, above and not beneath.

4. **Saved by grace** (Ephesians 2:8). Your past does not matter anymore. The blood of

Jesus has purified and justified you. You are redeemed and no more subject to guilt and condemnation. You are a child of God and a joint heir with Jesus Christ. You are seated with Christ in the heavenly places, far above principalities and powers. You are living a life of purpose now and can categorically reject temptations and refuse to bow to the things that once held you bound. Why? Because there is an overflow of God's grace upon you. You don't have to struggle to live right anymore because God's grace is sufficient for you!

5.  **Possessor of a sound mind.** 2 Timothy 1:7 says, "For God has not given us a spirit of fear, but of power and of love and of a sound mind." This means you are not dumb. You are not in any way abnormal. You have an excellent and productive mind. Your mind is a powerhouse of creativity and possibilities. Being an extract of divinity, your mind is loaded with potentials and possibilities. It is rich in powerful imaginations and revolutionary ideas that are waiting to be activated. In fact, there is really no limit to how much you can dream or to what length you can aspire in life.

6.  **More than a conqueror** (Romans 8: 37). That you are a child of God does not mean that battles, challenges and oppositions will not

come. But God says that, through it all, you are bound to prevail because you have the DNA of an overcomer in you. As long as you understand and activate the power in you, you will ever conquer fear, failure, sickness, limitations, oppositions, setbacks and any kind of attack from the enemy's camp.

Can you now see how important you really are? Can you see how precious and priceless you are in His sight? This is your true identity, hold it firmly and let no one tell you otherwise. Truth is, the moment you realize your self-worth, you begin to radiate God's glory, your joy will be limitless, you become more confident, bold, brave, indomitable, motivated, anointed, and fearless to step into your destiny and glow in greatness.

## YOUR IDENTITY AS A SHIELD

Having a true knowledge of your unique identity and exceeding worth will prevent you from needless worries. It will prevent you from falling into the snare of comparison that Satan has used to inflict dissatisfaction, confusion, frustration, depression and suicidal feelings upon many people.

Why do you think people sometimes feel worthless or suicidal? Most times, it's because they estimate their worth according to the standard or level of acceptance and approval of others. It is because they judge themselves according to the yardstick set by others, rather than looking inwards to appreciate their uniqueness and run their race according to the pace and standard set for them by God.

Here is the basic truth - until you begin to see and carry yourself as God sees you, you may never be able to do anything great in life. It's as simple as that. If you see yourself as someone irrelevant, then your mind (remember in chapter 1) plays the trick with negative thoughts and makes you believe in those negative thoughts and consequently, you become irrelevant!

But that's not all. If you don't define your identity and stay true to it, you will find that people will keep tossing you to and fro with their own ideas and agendas and you will end up feeling frustrated because you want to please everyone. That's the nature of humans for you, and if you leave the decision of your identity to them, you inevitably make yourself a candidate for failure.

## THE DECISION IS YOURS!

Remember, once again, that the way you see yourself is how others will see you too. So, create a perfect picture of yourself. Tell yourself every day how awesome you are; how beautiful, smart and blessed you are. Never think less of yourself.

Gone are the days when many of us fell prey to the lies of self-rejection, just because we felt we were nobody. Now we know that it is all a big lie.

It's a new dawn for you, friend. Believe in yourself, love and appreciate yourself, accept yourself the way you are and know for sure that you will not always remain the same. We learn and grow every day, each in his or her unique pace. It's one day at a time – you will definitely get to your destined pinnacle!

# THREE

## ATTITUDE & ALTITUDE – TWO INSEPERABLE TWINS

*"Jesus said to him, "If you can believe, all things are possible to him who believes."(Mark 9:23)*

I once read an inspiring story of a newspaper boy, whose reaction to a kindly comment made to him reveals a very important lesson on attitude. This boy, thinly clad and drenched by the rain, stood shivering in a doorway one cold winter's day, selling the newspapers. First, one bare foot and then the other was lifted for a moment and pressed against his leg to get a little warmth. Every few minutes, his piercing cry could be heard, "Morning paper! Morning paper!"

A man who was well protected by his coat and umbrella stopped to buy the early edition. Noting the boy's discomfort, he said, "This kind of weather is pretty hard on you, isn't it?" Looking up with a smile, the youngster replied, "I don't mind too much, Mister. The sun will shine again."

Young as that boy was, he had mastered one of the key secrets of winning in life – a positive mental attitude. And you can be sure that it would not be long before that boy would have gone higher to do greater things in life.

This is the reality of our existence here on earth. Life will not always give us what we deserve but what we demand. In other words, you cannot just sit by and expect life to be fair, just and good to you. No. You must know what you want and go for it with a winning attitude.

There are lots of riches and triumphs to enjoy in life; but the reality is that life does not yield its treasures easily. That's why you can't just find precious stones like diamonds, rubies, emeralds and the likes easily. You have to dig. If you don't want to dig, then you will have to settle for any of the common, almost worthless stones found easily on the surface of the earth.

Life does not guarantee any of us that we will not meet with difficulties, challenges and trials along the way. However, we can be sure of God's continued presence with us along the way for He said He will neither leave us nor forsake us

(Hebrews 13:5). Our attitude must be right, and it is that positive attitude that will help us to rise again much sooner than we think.

That's the way it goes with life generally – your expectations will determine your actualizations and your input will determine the output you get from it. As it is said in the world of computing – garbage in, garbage out!

Even God, in creating the universe, had to call forth what He wanted. The Scripture says, that in the beginning, "the earth was without form, and void; and darkness was on the face of the deep." (Genesis 1:2). God wasn't pleased with this and so He had to move into action – creating, shaping, sorting, structuring and evaluating – until He got exactly what He wanted. It was only then that He rested.

What is He telling you and me with this? Our attitude to life is the major determinant of what we get from it. As you can see from the example of God, you won't get the fullness of joy, peace, success, connection, greatness and breakthrough that you want by just wishing and daydreaming – you must take the bull by the horn and give yourself no rest until you are where you ought to be. In other words, if you want your dream to come true, you can't keep on dreaming; you must WAKE UP!

# WHAT EXACTLY IS ATTITUDE?

Attitude has been described as a settled way of thinking or feeling about something. It is, simply put, a frame of mind, a way of thinking, or a way of looking at things. In psychology, it is described as a psychological construct, a mental and emotional state that characterizes a person.

You can view attitude as a reflector, in that your attitude to life determines its attitude to you. This means that attitude is actually everything – or, the most important thing in life. Life isn't a bed of roses; there are times and seasons for everything, but your positive attitude will surely determine how far you get in life.

Ask yourself the following questions to assess your attitude:

- What does life mean to me?

- What is my attitude to life? Is it a positive one?

- What gets me up in the morning?

- What is my aim in life?

- Am I at the edge of giving up because things are not just working?

- If there are hindrances on my way, how do I handle them?

- When I see a need, do I strive to meet it?

- When I see a problem requiring a solution, do I actively seek the solution or do I leave it for "someone else"?

- Do I see a challenge in every opportunity or do I see an opportunity in every challenge?

If you can be sincere and honest with yourself with these questions, then you will understand what kind of attitude you have and why you are where you are today.

## WHY ATTITUDE IS EVERYTHING?

I stated earlier that attitude is everything. Let me explain a bit more about this. Since we have understood attitude to be a way of viewing things or viewing life in general, it goes without saying that you can either have a right or a wrong attitude, a good or a bad one. And, naturally, each comes with its own result. Simply put, you get what you look out for, whether it is in your outlook to life, relationship with God or interaction with your fellow men.

That, my friend, is why attitude is everything. It is what makes the difference between the optimist and the pessimist, the winner and the loser. It is what makes someone to believe the cup is half full, while the other thinks it's half empty. It is what differentiates the grateful from the ungrateful, the satisfied from the discontented, the one who enjoys a fulfilling relationship with God and man, and the one who seems frustrated with everybody.

## POSITIVE VERSUS NEGATIVE ATTITUDE

What all this means is that with a positive attitude, you already have the key to mastering life and getting the best from it. In fact, it begins to manifest in the way you view your own life. You will find yourself daily appreciating God for your existence, exploring your potentials, maximizing your strengths, neutralizing your weaknesses and consistently aiming for the best life that you can have. This is what Apostle Paul means when he says, "Not that I have already attained, or am already perfected; but I press on…I do not count myself to have apprehended; but one thing I do, forgetting those things which are behind and reaching forward to those things which are ahead" (Philippians 3:12-13).

That's exactly what people with a positive attitude do! They don't spend their entire life berating themselves, focusing on their weaknesses, nurturing their insecurities and magnifying their challenges. Rather, they PRESS ON, by daily relegating the negatives and celebrating the positives. This is how many great men and women become unstoppable in excellence and impact. It was not because they were perfect; it was because they handled their imperfections with the right attitude.

Not only do people with a positive attitude not waste their time whining about their inadequacies, but they also have the right reaction to criticism from others. They don't see criticism as a stumbling-block; they see it as a stepping-stone to greater heights. That's what happens to people with a positive attitude – they live an undefeated life because they just refuse to settle for less.

Why do you think the biblical David, despite his young age and not being a professional soldier, could confront Goliath, before whom even the best of Israel's warriors cringed in fear? The answer is that he had a positive mental attitude towards life. He had SUCCESS firmly engraved on his mind and that's all he could see and hear.

On the other hand, there have been several cases of people who should have succeeded and who even the world expected so much from but ended up not amounting to much in life – because they had a negative attitude towards themselves and others. They already programmed their minds to focus on failure and inadequacy and that's exactly what they got.

Myriads of beautiful things have been destroyed through a bad attitude. Many have lost great opportunities that could have transformed their lives because they chose to be negative in thinking and conduct. I once read of a job-seeker who was going for an interview and, out of frustration, picked a quarrel with a fellow passenger on the train and treated him badly. Shockingly for him, that same passenger was on the panel of interviewers for the job he was trying to get. Of course, the outcome of that interview can easily be guessed!

There have been cases of people already having great jobs but lost it through attitude issues. Many marriages have been wrecked and many destinies have been jeopardized because of negative attitudes. Perhaps the most touching example of how a wrong attitude can frustrate an otherwise glorious destiny is the case of the Israelites who perished in the wilderness. Despite the presence, power and promises of God with them; despite the many miracles they had encountered and the rare privileges they had, the vast majority of them still ended their lives in misery because of their decision to choose negativity and bitterness against God, instead of a positive attitude. The result was calamity for everyone involved.

# CHOOSE POSITIVITY

The good news for you, friend, is that no matter how things have been with you so far, you can choose to develop a positive attitude from today. Yes, you do have a choice, you can choose positivity over negativity at all times. Of course, there will be tough times but your approach can make things right again. Nick Vujicic said, "We may have absolutely no control over what happens to us, but we can control how we respond. If we choose the right attitude, we can rise above whatever challenges we face." Be wise and be the change you want in your life. Be positive!

# FOUR

## FOLLOW YOUR PASSION

*"Before I formed you in the womb I knew you;*
*Before you were born I sanctified you; I ordained you a*
*prophet to the nations."(Jeremiah 1:5)*

———————— ⊛ ————————

What is your passion? Your passion is any activity that you have a natural interest in. It is what comes from deep within you and fills you with unusual energy and enthusiasm. You do it effortlessly. You do it with joy. This activity needs no external motivation because it naturally challenges and motivates you. It drives you and inspires you to take risks and go beyond your current limit.

Passion comes in many forms. Yours could be teaching others, relating with children, caring for others, fixing things, building gadgets, debating, acting, singing, advocating for justice, motivating others, seeking solution to health puzzles, caring for pets or plants, gardening, reading, writing, doing artistic works, sporting activities, handicraft, body grooming, decorations, fashion design and so on.

It is important that you discover your passion because it is a key pointer to your calling, purpose and destiny. So, in case you have been wondering what exactly your purpose in life is, look closely again at your passion – what gives you that instant drive and excitement just thinking of it – and you are likely to discover your ultimate purpose. As Bishop T.D Jakes rightly notes, "If you can't figure out your purpose, figure out your passion. For your passion will lead you right into your purpose."

To achieve anything in life, passion must come first. Think of great leaders, and you will be struck by their passion: Pastor E. Adeboye for Ministry, Nnamdi Azikwe for one Nigeria, Gandhi for human rights, Churchill for freedom, Martin Luther King Jr. for equality, Bill Gates for technology, Mother Teresa for service to the poor, Robert W. Woodruff for coke at every table and others.

These men live beyond an ordinary life and have great desire to make a difference. Call it passion, commitment or conviction. Whatever the name, powerful leaders have it in large measure. They also insist on sharing it, constantly. Their passion is not directionless. It is sharply focused around what they want to achieve. It is concentrated and, like a laser beam, cuts through objections, obstacles and negativity. It is hard to say no to someone who cares so strongly about something and difficult to resist being drawn into their vision and becoming engaged.

## FINDING YOUR PASSION

Determining that activity that gives you the greatest joy is of utmost importance. According to Heather Monahan, founder of a career mentoring group, "To truly reach your potential, you need to identify your passions and talents and create ways to utilize them each day." Of course, you may discover that there is more than one activity that you are passionate about, but if you take your time to analyze these activities, you will discover that your degrees of interest are not the same. Your true passion will always fill you with more joy and enthusiasm than others. In my case, I've always had a passion for different activities, including fashion, music, adventure and entrepreneurship. Along the line, I discovered my true passion and I followed it. Sure, I still sing, I still love fashion, I'm an entrepreneur, and I love adventures.

Four things have helped me to find fulfillment all along: FINDING my passion, FOCUSING on it, LEARNING to develop it, and then EXPLORING its numerous possibilities.

Couldn't find your passion at first and you gave up after few days? Arise, keep trying, and you'll find it eventually, if you will not give in.

Thought you found your passion but you got tired of it? Not to worry! Start over again and find a new passion. There may be more than one passion in your lifetime, so explore all the possibilities.

Found your passion but haven't been successful making a living at it? Don't give up. Keep trying, and try again, until you succeed. Success doesn't come easy, so giving up early is a sure way to fail. Keep trying, and you'll get there.

Generally, there are noticeable characteristics of a passion, which can help you pinpoint yours:

- Great excitement and love come with a passion.

- When you are engaged in this activity, you are not bothered about time.

- You are always eager and looking forward to every opportunity to engage in it.

- You find yourself proactive with great flow of ideas.

- You are at peace and also satisfied simply because you love what you are doing.

- It introduces you to like-minded and positive people.

- You leverage any opportunity when it surfaces.

- You are more confident and more hardworking.

- You are usually proud of your achievement.

Remember also that your purpose and passion are interwoven and each can lead to the other. So, create some time to look within yourself and you will certainly discover your passion!

There are no two ways about it. If you strongly want anything, you can find the willpower to achieve it. The only way to have that kind of desire and willpower is to develop passion.

Career experts and counselors have often advised that rather than choosing a job for the money or prestige, it is better to choose it for your happiness. And there really shouldn't be a detachment between your passion and your career. In fact, connecting your career with your passion will give you the best satisfaction. This is why it is often said that "if you love what you do, you will never work a day in your life."

Of course, you can be engaged in a profession while doing your passion by the side. However, it is advisable that you discover your passion early and then begin to channel your career path around it.

## WHY YOU MUST FOLLOW YOUR PASSION

Finding and following your passion is deeply rewarding. Your passion and career path may not necessarily be something that people consider lucrative or prestigious, but don't forget that this is strictly about you. Your destiny is unique to you and what brings you joy does not necessarily have to conform to other people's standard.

So, whatever your passion is, "do it with all your might" (Ecclesiastes 10:10). Don't let people make you feel inferior because of your passion or chosen career path. You know what you are doing and why you are doing it – that's the most important thing, since you are solely responsible for finding happiness in life. Many people who are being celebrated today for making the most of their passions once faced opposition and rejection (sometimes in very severe forms), but as they stuck to what they believed in, their former critics have turned out to be their greatest fans.

Sadly, there have been instances when some people have allowed themselves to be pressured into giving up their passions, or chasing after money at the expense of their interests. In the end, it was all a tale of dissatisfaction and regret. This was why the late Myles Munroe once declared that the wealthiest place on earth is not any of the countries rich in mineral or petroleum resources but the CEMETERY. According to him, "It is because in the cemetery are books that were never written, painting that no wall will ever see...the graveyard is filled with music that no one has ever heard and poetry that no one will ever read, ideas that will never be reality; the cemetery is filled with great men that died as alcoholics and drug addicts; it is filled with powerful women that died as prostitutes; it is filled with dreams that will never come to pass; it is filled with businesses that will never open. What a tragedy!"

I pray that your situation does not end this way. You have only one life to live – make the most of it. Do all you are meant to do; be all you are meant to be!

# FIVE

## YOU NEED GOALPOSTS

*"I press toward the goal for the prize of the upward call of God..." (Philippians 3:14)*

———— ✦ ————

Have you ever wondered why those two vertical posts at each end of a soccer pitch are called goalposts? It is because that's where each of the competing teams are supposed to be directing their efforts. The goalpost therefore performs a number of functions simultaneously – it lets the teams know the direction they should be playing, the direction they should not be playing, when to be motivated, when to be happy, when to be sad, when they have fouled (offside etc.) and when they have won. In other words, it generally makes the entire game meaningful, purposeful and worthwhile.

Now imagine what will happen if there are no

goalposts. It means anything goes. Not only will there be no rules or meaningful purpose and motivation for the players, but the entire exercise becomes tiring and frustrating. This is exactly what happens to a person who has no goals. Initially, it may appear that one is having fun as there is nothing much to task one's mind and body, but sooner or later, everything becomes meaningless.

Without goals, not only will frustration set in as there is no way to measure the success of your efforts but the passion and enthusiasm for living will soon fizzle out, as there are no rules to govern your life and no joy of accomplishment. Goals are the targets that drive and stretch us. They are objectives that you seek to accomplish from time to time and in the long run. They give direction to your efforts and wings to your passion. They help you to evaluate your life to determine areas requiring correction and improvement, thereby making you a better person.

Goals are very important to your life. Before you can be called a success, there must have been a target for you to achieve; before you can accomplish something, you must know exactly what you want and be sure that it is what pursuing.

This is a major secret of the successful people that we celebrate today. They are goal-driven; they keep setting newer and higher goals for themselves. This, by the way, is the whole essence of our existence – to keep reaching out for new horizons and possibilities, until we become all that God has created us to be. Without this, life easily loses its flavor.

Note very importantly that while it is crucial to set goals for your life as a whole, it is also necessary to set goals in each area of your life, because the purpose of God for you is to prosper, flourish, excel and be the best you can be in every area of your life (3 John 2). Thus you can set goals in your spiritual life, career, finance, relationship, marriage, business, health and so on. Besides, your goals can be short-term (daily, weekly, monthly) or long-term, spanning years.

Regardless of the area of life in which you are setting the goal, certain characteristics mark out a good goal and facilitate its accomplishment. Our Lord Jesus Christ says, "For which of you, intending to build a tower, does not sit down first and count the cost, whether he has enough to finish it" (Luke 14:28).

Therefore, a good goal must:

- Be a product of thorough thinking - not done for doing's sake.

- Strategic - designed to achieve a specific, noticeable objective.

- Stretch you – makes you step out of your comfort zone.

- Have the capacity to make you a better person.

- Be able to drive you to greater self-discovery, self-awareness and self-confidence.

All these lessons are subsumed in the "SMART" principle of goal-setting. SMART is an acronym containing the widely accepted features of an effective goal. Put simply, you will find your goals working wonders in your life if they are:

- **S - SPECIFIC:** Your goals have to be exact, precise and well-defined. What exactly do you want to achieve? Don't set general goals like "I want to be a better person" – identify the particular area or areas in which you want to be better. Again, don't just say "I want to lose weight" – state how much weight you want to shed within a given period of time. Part of being specific is also stating why the goal is important, who needs to be part of it, what you need to put in place, when you need to start and where it is meant to start. You need to be very detailed.

- **M - MEASURABLE:** This goes along with being specific. If your goals are not specific, they cannot be measurable. Being measurable means that the yardstick for tracking progress is included in setting the goal. In other words, your goal should be set in such a way that you will clearly know once it is accomplished. For instance, rather than saying "I want to develop my vocabulary and become more fluent in the English Language," you can say "I will finish, at least, one novel or motivational book every two weeks and write out at least ten new words I have learned from it." This way, it is much easier to track your progress at the end of each specified period.

- **A - ACHIEVABLE:** This has to do with being realistic in setting your goal. Note that, with goal-setting, what matters most is that you are making progress, not becoming all you wish to become overnight. So, even though your goals must be challenging (otherwise they are useless) they must also be set with due consideration of your ability and other necessary factors. For instance, if, as a salary-earner who has a family, you want to save towards buying a new car or house, the amount you will decide to save monthly and the time frame you will give yourself must be with due consideration of the basic needs of the family that are non-negotiable.

- **R - RELEVANT:** For a goal to be motivating, it must be meaningful. What ensures this meaningfulness is the relevance of the goal to your life. You have to ask yourself: Is this goal relevant to me? Is this the right time for it? Will it be worth it at the end? How will it impact lives positively? Why do I want to reach this goal? What are the main objectives behind it? These are the questions you need to ask yourself.

- **T - TIME-BOUND:** Time matters in achieving your goals. In fact, without being time-bound - that is, having a set time within which it must have been accomplished – a goal has failed from the start. So, give your goal a deadline, set a target and run with it. Keep the time realistic as much as possible.

## STEPS FOR ACCOMPLISHMENT

Having a great goal that meets all the requirements of goal-setting is good, but beyond that is the accomplishment. Not all well-structured goals are accomplished. The reason is simple – even the best of goals cannot accomplish itself; it needs human commitment. Apparently then, you need, in addition to your goals, the following:

**1. A plan of action.** Each of your goals must be accompanied by a plan of action that will lead to its accomplishment. This is the "how" of your goal. So, it is not enough to specific with your goal, you should also specify HOW you want to accomplish it. Remember, the first step towards getting somewhere is to decide that you are not going to stay where you are.

**2. Determination.** Determination is when you desire to do something so much without allowing anyone or any difficulties to stop you from doing it. This definition could not be any more accurate and that is what the beauty of determination is and why it's so important for anyone to have. Without determination, you will give up easily in the face of difficulties. Everyone can achieve something if they are willing to put in the work and have a determination towards overcoming the particular challenge and people who doubt their ability to achieve greatness. That's the power of determination and having that by your side can make a difference to your life.

Most times, we struggle to make our goals a reality. Yes, why the struggle? It's often because we allow wrong ideas, bad influence, wrong timing, wrong approach, circumstances, finance, lackadaisical attitude, procrastination, fear and other factors to limit us. I once had my fair share of these. However, through it all, the most important thing I did for myself was to never give up!

So, no matter how hard it seems for you to achieve

your goals, do not give up on yourself because God will never give up on you! Knowing that God will never give up on you alone is more than enough relief. Therefore, if you try and fail, try again and again!

**3. Discipline.** It's never easy to stretch oneself to be more or to do more. The "comfort zone" always seems so sweet with its limited demands. So, it will take a lot of discipline for you to shun the good and seek the better. There will be temptations, distractions and discomforts. But through it all, keep your eyes on the joy of accomplishment. As it is said of our Lord Jesus Christ, "...who for the joy that was set before Him endured the cross, despising the shame, and has sat down at the right hand of the throne of God" (Hebrews 12:2). Be focused and always remind yourself to take that step; as you pursue it, you are getting closer to achieving it.

Finally, bear in mind to set high goals and dream big dreams. Be prayerful, consistent, full of radical faith, proactive, dedicated, committed, industrious and self-controlled. Keep learning and pushing; break out of your comfort zone, make that great sacrifice. Is there room for mistakes? Yes, there will always be mistakes. I've made countless mistakes myself and I am glad that happened because it contributed to making me who I am today. Yes, mistakes make you stronger and wiser. Learn from them and move on.

The point is, whatever you do, don't stop working on yourself and moving FORWARD!

# SIX

## YOUR TIME, YOUR LIFE

*"Be very careful, then, how you live—not as unwise but as wise, making the most of every opportunity…"* *(Ephesians 5:15-16, NIV).*

———————— ❦ ————————

Central to the accomplishment of your goals is the management of your time. And it is important that we talk about this, especially in these days of countless cable TV channels, soap operas, sitcoms, smartphone apps and games, and worst of all, social media – all with contents jostling for our time. In fact, as the BBC reported recently, things have gotten so bad that researchers are looking into classifying social media addiction as a mental disorder because it seems so rampant. Yes, it may sound funny but it is one of the stark realities of the period in which we live – and a major reason you must consciously determine to make the most of your time.

One of the most productive skills you can have in life is effective time management. Our life on earth is composed of time; which means that if you can manage your time well, you can easily manage your life. Time management has been defined as "the process of planning and exercising conscious control of time spent on specific activities, especially to increase effectiveness, efficiency, and productivity." This "conscious control" tallies with the revelation in Ecclesiastes 3:1 that "To everything there is a season, a time for every purpose under heaven."

When you manage your time well, it enables you to work smarter, speedily and more easily. Sometimes we wonder why despite the fact that everyone has 24 hours each day, some people seem to achieve so much each day – so much that they end each day with the joy of accomplishment – while some others achieve so little and end each day lamenting the "shortness of time". The answer is in the way time is managed.

Having understood how essential it is for me to have consistent and effective time management, I have designed a personal timetable for every day of the week. Time is precious and priceless, so I ensure that every minute of my day is invested, not just spent. I have time for studying, time for meditation, time for leisure, time for prayer and so on. This is a habit I have maintained from my school days, and I can testify that it has tremendously guided, guarded and galvanized me on the path of achieving my set goals.

The essence of time management is for you to discipline yourself to set clear priorities, and then to stick to those priorities. You must consciously and deliberately select the most valuable and important thing that you could be doing at any given time, and then discipline yourself to work solely on that task.

In your personal life, you goal is to get the highest "return on energy" from your activities. Ken Blanchard refers to this as getting the highest "return on life."

Just as you would be careful about investing your money to assure that you get the highest rate of return, you must be equally as careful when you invest your time. You must be sure that you earn the highest level of results, rewards and satisfaction from the limited amount of time you have.

Always, before you commit to a time consuming activity, you must ask, "Is this the very best use of my time?"

Lack of self-discipline in time management leads people to procrastinate continually on their top tasks, leading them to spend more and more time on task of low-value or no-value. And whatever you do repeatedly eventually becomes a habit.

I'm sure that you too would be more concerned about the way you spend your time if you can have a full understanding of how valuable and critical time is to your life and the fulfillment of your destiny. Here is an interesting illustration on this. Suppose you had a bank that freely credited your account every morning with $1,440, and every evening cancelled whatever part of the amount you failed to use during the day, what would you do? Of course, you would draw out every cent daily and use it to your advantage!

Well, you may not know it but you have such a bank already, and its name is TIME! Every morning it credits you with 1440 minutes. Every night it rules off as lost whatever of this you failed to invest to good purpose. It carries over no balances, it allows no overdrafts. Each day it opens a new account with you. If you fail to use the day's deposits, the loss is yours. There is no going back. There is no drawing against tomorrow.

I hope you have a better picture of the value of your time now. And as I said before, in this case, there is no partiality; everyone (male or female, young or old, rich or poor) is credited with an equal amount of time every morning. From then on, every second, minute and hour begin to expire, never to be regained. I mean NEVER to be regained. This is why the Scripture counsels, "Be very careful, then, how you live—not as unwise but as wise, making the most of every opportunity…" (Ephesians 5:15-16, NIV).

What the Scripture urges here is that you should be more conscious of maximizing your time, instead of "killing" it. See, you cannot kill time without doing some harm to your life, however imperceptible it may seem. You know why? Within the same time that some people are "killing", several others are making millions, impacting lives, transforming destinies, influencing their communities, and fulfilling their passions. This is why you must, like Moses, pray to God, "So teach us to number our days, that we may gain a heart of wisdom" (Psalm 90:12).

## TIME MANAGEMENT TIPS

Okay, enough of theories now, let's get more practical. How can you manage your time to get the most of it?

### 1. Set Your Goals Right

I cannot over-emphasize this. Good time-management begins with a well-planned day with clearly outlined goals. As we discussed in the last chapter, when there are no goals, anything goes. This is the number one reason why many of us are so prone to time-wasting. We have no detailed plan of how each moment of our day will be spent. Naturally, we become vulnerable to time-killers. To avoid this, you can decide before going to bed each night to plan your schedule of activities for the next day. Once this is done, it becomes easier for you to get going once the new day dawns.

Your daily plan should always revolve around perfecting and continuously working on tasks related to your goals. Setting your goal the right way helps in avoiding unnecessary hitches. It is helpful to set your goals using the SMART principle, as discussed earlier.

## 2. Observe the 80/20 Rule (or the law of the vital few)

This is one of the most important principles you must pay attention to because it has the potential to transform the way you manage your time and significantly boost your productivity. The rule is also called the Pareto Principle, after its founder, the Italian economist Vilfredo Pareto. Pareto had observed that people in society seemed to divide naturally into what he called the "vital few," or the top 20 percent in terms of money and influence, and the "trivial many," or the bottom 80 percent. He further noticed that virtually all economic activity was subject to this principle, in that 80 percent of the wealth of Italy during that time was controlled by 20 percent of the population.

Overtime, this analysis by Pareto has been found to be true in all areas of life, especially in business, productivity and time-management. Specifically for daily time management, you will find that 20 percent of your daily activities will account for 80 percent of your satisfying accomplishments in the day. The remaining 80 percent fall into the category of minor or negligible activities. Sadly, most people tend to focus on these negligible activities (often because they seem easier and more fun) only to find out at the end of the day that they haven't achieved anything tangible.

The trick in the Pareto principle therefore is to identify these "vital few" activities that produce the real results for you and give them priority attention. Why? Because they matter a lot and the satisfaction you get from accomplishing them will easily override the thought of the other 80 percent you might not have had much time for. This is the easiest way to make the most of your 24 hours. Prioritize. Put first things first and the rest will be easily sorted!

## 3. Avoid Distractions

When you cannot pay attention to the important things you are supposed to be doing, it means you are being distracted. And I'm sure that, if you would be sincere enough, you probably already know what your distractions are. So, go ahead and deal with them. Yes, it may feel good to keep them around, but don't forget how much of your life you are losing in exchange for whatever you're getting in return. As someone rightly says, "Your time keeps flying away into vanity while you dine with your distractions. Your life keeps diminishing while you waste your time feeding your distractions."

To overcome distractions, observe the following:

- Have a well-planned timetable for yourself.

- Get a small corner desk around your house for your work.

- Turn off your cellphone and the TV, and stay off the Internet, if need be.

- Get a good sleep and be relaxed.

- Be disciplined.

- Even if some people feel offended that you no longer waste your time with them, remain focused on your goal.

- Assess your accomplishments at the end of each day. Tick off goals achieved and find out what prevented you from achieving the rest (the important goals, that is). Then strategize on how to improve.

## 4. Plan Ahead

Planning is very much necessary. As with other areas of life, in time-management, he who fails to plan has already planned to fail. Planning gives you enough time to think about great ideas; it makes you proactive. Planning ahead builds your confidence, makes you productive and ultimately gives you outstanding results.

Another simple method of time management that you can use to overcome procrastination requires self-discipline, will-power and personal organization, but by using this system, you can double and triple your productivity, performance and output.

Start by making a list of everything you have to do each day, before you begin. As stated above, best time to make this list is the evening before, at the end of the workday, so that your subconscious mind can work on your list of activities while you sleep. You will often wake up with ideas and insights on how to more effectively complete the tasks of the day.

Apply the A B C D E Method to your list:

**A** = "Must do" – Serious consequences for non-completion;

**B** = "Should do" – Mild consequences for doing or not doing;

**C** = "Nice to do" – No consequences whether you do it or not;

**D** = "Delegate" – Everything you possibly can to free up more time for those things that only you can do;

**E** = "Eliminate" – Discontinue all tasks and activities that are no longer essential to your work and to achieving your goals.

It takes tremendous self-discipline to select your most important task, and then to start on that task rather than doing anything else. But once you begin work on it, you will start to feel a flow of energy that motivates and propels you into the task. You will feel more positive and confident. You will feel excited and happy. The very act of starting on an important task raises your self-esteem and motivates you to continue.

Deep within each person is an intense desire to feel strong, effective, powerful and in control of his or her life. You automatically trigger these feelings of self-confidence and self-esteem when you start to work on the task that is most important to you at the moment.

When I have any work to do, I take my time to plan thoroughly before the set date. Tell you what? It makes the bulk of the work much super-duper easier. I encourage you to do same and you will notice the huge difference it will make in your life.

Starting today, you should apply these key time management principles to every area of your life. Apply them to your work, your family, your health, your exercise routine and your financial decisions and activities.

# SEVEN

## WHO ARE YOUR FRIENDS?

*"He who walks with wise men will be wise, But the companion of fools will be destroyed" (Proverbs 13:20)*

———————— ⟡ ————————

Here again is another issue we cannot ignore on our quest for greatness and fulfillment of destiny. Make no mistake about it: The people you often surround yourself with have a lot of influence on your life. Or to put it simply, your circle of friends will determine how far you will go in life. If, for instance, you surround yourself with frivolous, immoral and negative-minded friends, you will sooner or later end up being like them - thinking like them, acting like them, craving what they love and compromising God's purpose for your life. This is why the Bible says, "He who walks with wise men will be wise, but the companion of fools will be destroyed" (Proverbs 13:20).

Friendship indeed plays a vital role in all spheres of our lives (socially, mentally, physically, emotionally, spiritually and so on) and it can also directly influence our moods, feelings and dispositions about life. Greatness thrives on positivity; so the kind of companions you need are those who will constantly inspire you to think and pursue excellence in all areas of your life.

The Bible says "Iron sharpens iron" (Proverbs 27:17) – that in itself is a basic truth of life. There is no way wood will sharpen iron; rather it will make it blunt. This means that you can never achieve much in life with the shackling weight and negative influence of friendship that only thrives on gossiping, complaining and time-wasting. This is why you must strive to build around yourself a strong circle of positive-minded friends that will help you attain great heights and fulfill your destiny. According to Jim Rohn, "You are the average of the five people you spend the most time with."

## PAINS OF NEGATIVE FRIENDSHIP

Many have taken the above advice on friendship for granted and have had to pay dearly for it. Recently, I read of a Nigerian lady who had some private pictures of hers posted on the social media. The pictures attracted lots of humiliating comments, not only to the lady but to her entire family. But the most shocking aspect was not the pictures or the comments but the identity of the poster which many did not know initially. However, a few weeks after the incident, the affected lady summoned up the courage to react to the pictures and here's what she said:

"The past few days have been some of the most challenging and traumatic days of my life following the invasion of my privacy by my supposed friends. I have taken note of the diverse comments that trailed the pictures posted on the social media and I'm most grateful to the intelligent and discerning social media users who were quick to note the evil and mischievous intentions of my so called friends…I have admittedly learnt some hard facts of life which have marked a turning point in my life…"

Instructively, one of the hard facts that this lady learned, in her exact words, is: "Your choice of friends can either make or mar your destiny." Well, it is sad that our friend learned this fact of life the hard way. But you cannot wait for such an experience before you learn. And this is why you must begin to re-evaluate the kinds of people you currently surround yourself with, so you can decide those to do away with before they do away with your dignity and destiny.

# GAINS OF POSITIVE FRIENDSHIP

On the other hand, there have been many cheering stories of people who received massive help (moral and financial), discovered their purpose, overcame their weaknesses, bounced back from failure, recovered from heartbreaks, achieved outstanding feats and attained incredible heights through the backing of true friends who were there for them through thick and thin. This is why the Bible says, *"A man who has friends must himself be friendly, But there is a friend who sticks closer than a brother"* (Proverbs 18:24).

In this regard, we have some scriptural examples – the most popular of which, arguably, was that of David and Jonathan. David and Jonathan were from different family backgrounds but they formed a solid friendship, driven by mutual loyalty and sacrificial love. Each benefited from the other immensely. Indeed, after Jonathan's death, David still went ahead to show uncommon favor to Jonathan's crippled son, Mephibosheth (2 Samuel 9). There was also the friendship of Paul and Barnabas, which not only nurtured the growth and edification of each of the friends but also enabled them to carry out great exploits together.

All these positive examples, as well as the negative ones that we previously considered, go a long way to prove the truth of the observation of the lady in our first illustration: Your choice of friends can either make or mar your destiny!

## SO, WHO IS A FRIEND?

In describing a true friend and why you need one, let me refer you to some of the definitions submitted when a British publication decided to offer a prize for the best definition of a friend. Among the thousands of answers received were the following:

- "One who multiplies joys, divides grief, and whose honesty is inviolable."

- "One who understands our silence."

- "A volume of sympathy bound in cloth."

- "A watch that beats true for all time and never runs down."

The winning definition read:

- "A friend is the one who comes in when the whole world has gone out."

Now that you have a good picture of who a friend should be, take some time to consider the circle of friends you have and ask yourself these key questions:

- Who do I spend most of my time with?

- How do they make me feel?

- Are they assets or liabilities, pillars or caterpillars?

- Are they inspiring and encouraging me to be better?

- Have they in any way motivated or impacted my life positively?

- Are they always honest and sincere with me?

- Do they offer helpful criticism, even if I don't want to hear it, or do they flatter me even when I'm in the wrong?

- Do they understand my life's purpose and are they capable of helping me achieve it?

The answers you provide to these questions will determine whether you are on course to greatness with your current circle of friends or whether you are going the opposite direction.

## CHARACTER TRAITS OF HELPFUL FRIENDS

Like precious stones, true friends are hard to find, but when you find one, you will certainly know. How do you identify a true friend?

- They are caring.

- They bring out the best in you – they help you discover and fire up your hidden potentials.

- They are non-judgmental.

- They listen more and talk less.

- They are always happy and fun to be with.

- They inspire and support you.

- They are honest, open and real.

- They look for ways to study and pray with you.

- They are confident and loyal.

- They love challenges.

- They love to think outside the box.

- They take a deep interest in your wellbeing.

- They encourage, motivate and push you towards being successful.

- They are not complainers but problem-solvers.

Positive friends have a huge impact on your success and happiness; they give you confidence, make you feel valued and offer support and love when needed. Friends are special because each one is unique, but there are common factors that make a positive friend.

Good friends are meant to pick you up when you are down, as well as give compliments and congratulate you when you have achieved something special. They genuinely share your happiness when you succeed, and are the first ones to suggest you celebrate. They are also sensitive when you are upset or disappointed and cheer you on until you are back on your feet.

Good friends, more than anything, make you feel happy and raise your self-esteem. If your friends regularly make you feel down about yourself, your accomplishments and your ambitions, it might be time to move on.

Real positive friends are the real deal and the real gems. They are always optimistic and help to boost your morale and self-esteem. They want you to be happy and will go out of their way to help you when you're feeling down or need special attention.

On the other hand, negative friends, as we have seen, celebrate the downfall of others, and as a result, you'll end up feeling worse about yourself or your situation. They are jealous and have no value to add to you.

So, if you want to be successful and great in life, surround yourself with friends who are go-getters, motivators, positive-thinkers, shakers and movers.

Hold them close. They will give you energy and help you create the success you want and deserve." Positive people are great. They feel good about themselves and life in general. They are enthusiastic – and their enthusiasm is contagious. When you surround yourself with positive people, you'll become more positive and enthusiastic too. Note again: Your circle of friends determines how far you can go in life. You have the power to choose; so, choose wisely!

# EIGHT

## ACTIVATE YOUR NEXT LEVEL

*"And the Lord said to Moses,. "Why do you cry to Me? Tell the children of Israel to go FORWARD." (Exodus 14:15)*

———————— ✦ ————————

Let me congratulate you – your time to move on to the next level has come!

But first, you must do a sincere self-assessment of the key areas of your life – spiritual, academic, financial, relationship (or marriage), professional, emotional, social and mental. Where are you now? How long have you been here? Are you still in the same condition you've always been for the past few years? Are you happy with where you are right now? Can you boldly pat yourself on the back and say you are proud of whom you've become? Are you doing what you should be doing?

If your answers to these questions are positive, great! But know that this is just the beginning. God's desire for you is that you continue to "prosper and be in health, even as your soul prospers" (3 John 2). So, you must continue to advance towards perfection; towards being the best you can be. Never give room to complacency because, "he who stops being better stops being good."

On the other hand, if your answers to the assessment questions are not satisfactory enough, do not despair. Indeed, the fact that you feel dissatisfied is a sign of hope. As I said earlier, it is, in fact, the first step towards making progress. But mere acknowledgement and disapproval of your condition won't do – you must ACT!

Moses declared to the Israelites in Deuteronomy 1:6-8: "The LORD our God spoke to us in Horeb, saying: 'You have dwelt long enough at this mountain. Turn and take your journey, and go to the mountains of the Amorites, to all the neighboring places in the plain, in the mountains and in the lowland, in the South and on the seacoast, to the land of the Canaanites and to Lebanon, as far as the great river, the River Euphrates. See, I have set the land before you; go in and possess the land which the LORD swore to your fathers…"

That is exactly what God expects you to do. It is not enough for you to visualize where you should be and keep regretting why you have not been there. This won't change anything because it contradicts the very first law of motion. Remember it? "Everything continues in a state of rest unless it is compelled to change by forces impressed upon it." So, rather than merely wishing, set the forces of progress in motion by making a move (however little it may be) towards your desired destination.

## DON'T LET YOUR SITUATION STOP YOU!

In Matthew 20 we find the story of two blind men waiting just outside the city of Jericho. Blind – could not see a thing! Wandering with hands outstretched at times, trying to find their way through life. Not a great CONDITION to be in. But somehow they found out that Jesus was passing their direction. They immediately began calling out to Him, endeavoring to get His attention, putting themselves in position for an encounter with the One who could make a radical difference in their lives. And when they called out to him, they did so with anticipation of His favor!

They called out to the Son of David – Messiah. Even though their condition was dark, their position was that the one who could make a difference was close by, and would change their world forever! He came to them and can you believe it – asked them "What do you want me to do for you?" "Well" said one of them, "I've got this neighbor who has a great aunt whose mother is…" No way! "We want to see", they replied! And Jesus touched their eyes and immediately, their condition matched their position!

So, what's your condition? You may not be physically blind, but you find yourself in a fog seemingly reaching out to try to make your way along. Don't let your present condition define your position! You are more than a conqueror – You are a new creature – You have been given power to become as a Child of God!

## PERSONAL EXPERIENCE

I was once at a stage in my life where I was completely sad simply because I felt totally stuck. Nothing seemed to be working out the way I wanted it and I spent some time lamenting my situation. One day, however, I woke up and I shook off the "pity-party" feeling. I looked at my image in the mirror and said to myself, "Enough is enough!"

Then, I went into action. I started by asking

myself, "Okay, now, what do I do next? How can I improve on myself?" I carefully took down some notes on what I needed to do to become a better version of who I was back then. And I can tell you that once I took that decision and got into action, it was as if the floodgates of transformation were opened before me and my life has never been the same since then. Yes, it took some work, pains and radical choices. But I tell you that it's been worth it all the way.

Never let your condition define or confine you. You can be whatever you want to be whenever you desire it so. I ask you, who says you can't get that job? Who says you are ugly? Who says you are incompetent? Who says you can't start that business? Who says there is no other way? Who says it's the end for you? Who says you can't be successful? Who says you can't' achieve your dream? Who says WHAT???

Look, if you allow your present condition, past failures or people's opinions to define you, you will eventually have yourself to blame. That's the truth. Of course, it may appear that your dreams are already shattered and your hopes dashed, but it's not the end of the world for you. The God of the "dry bones" in Ezekiel 37 is still on the throne and is willing to partner with you to turn your life around. If He could make multitudes of bones that had been very dry, scattered and jumbled to be sorted out, come together and become living souls, then your situation cannot be an impossible one for Him. All He requires from you (as He required from Ezekiel) is to believe and to act!

Again, I say to you, never accept your present condition as your final destination. Say to yourself: "I am more than a conqueror!"; "Yes I can!"; "I am fearfully and wonderfully made!"; "I am a light that must shine!"; "I am a success!"; "I have the power of God in me, therefore, I walk without fear!"

God, in Jeremiah 29:11 says, "For I know the thoughts that I think toward you…thoughts of peace and not of evil, to give you a future and a hope." Did you see that? Regardless of your present, there is a FUTURE for you – and a glorious one at that. This Bible passage alone is enough to build your confidence in God and trust in Him and not your ability. Often, problems and confusion arise because we are trying to do God's work for him. Let God do what He alone can do. That's why He is GOD!

## NEVER TOO LATE

By the way, who says it is too late for you to pursue that dream, make that change or right that wrong? It's all a myth. So, quit regretting and start living.

Everyone's situation is different but what is the same, is that to make this change, you need to stay determined and always have a positive, never give up attitude. I am are not saying that it is going to be easy, but if it is what you want, then your hard work will pay off and you will thank yourself down the track that you made this choice. No pain, no gain!

I have heard cheering testimonies of people who, due to parental pressure, peer pressure or some other reasons studied the wrong course in a tertiary institution, only for them to return several years later and study their desired course, sometimes even graduating with the best result. So, who says it is too late for you to get that qualification that will make you a perfect fit for the career you really want?

What is stopping you from pursuing your passion? Who says it is too late for you? If everyone thinks it is over for you, why should you think same? Susan Boyle once said, "There are enough people in the world who are going to write you off. You don't need to do that to yourself." And of course, she was very much qualified to say such, having had her fair share of ridicule and criticism from people who never expected her to amount to much in her quest to be a singer. She was already 47 when she participated in "Britain's Got Talent" and many mocked her when she announced on the show that her dream was to become one of the most famous musicians in history. She didn't have the looks or the youthfulness they had expected, but she wasn't bothered. You know what? Not only did she excel at the competition but the album she released later that year became the UK's best-selling debut album of all time. Yes, you read that well – bestselling not only for that year but for all time. And she was almost 50!

But there are even more inspiring examples. Laura Ingalls Wilder had been a teacher and farmer at different times in her life, until the age of 43 when her daughter encouraged her to write an autobiography. Her initial attempts did not impress publishers but she refused to give up and continued to improve on her writing skills. She was 65 years old when her book "Little House in the Big Woods" was published and it became a mega success. She would go ahead to write other "Little House" series including the last one that came out when she was 76 years old!

How about Anna Mary Robertson Moses (popularly known as Grandma Moses) who only began painting series of artistic works in her 70s? Her big break came when an art collector saw some of her works in a local store and bought them all. She was 78 then and soon became an international success. At that old age, she appeared on magazine covers, on television stations, and in a documentary of her life. She wrote an autobiography (My Life's History), won numerous awards, and was awarded two honorary doctoral degrees. The New York Times would later say of her: "The simple realism, nostalgic atmosphere and luminous color with which Grandma Moses portrayed simple farm life and rural countryside won her a wide following…"

There are several other examples of "never-say-never" champions that I can cite, but the question again is: what is YOUR excuse?

All of these amazing people achieved their dreams because they believed in themselves. Others definitely tried to influence and dissuade them from pursuing their aspirations but they were successful because they kept the dream alive, they continued chasing dreams.

What are you capable of? Don't doubt living the life you dream of; it is within your reach. Start working toward your dream today, don't allow it to die!

## IT'S YOUR TURN

It is time for action, dear friend. Yes, time to begin the process of turning your life around. Start by thinking of what needs to be changed, adjusted, polished, replaced, revived and thrashed in your life. Start working right away. Now is the time for a rebirth of your person. It's never too late to begin rebuilding your life and make it fantastically amazing.

This is not the time for focusing on the past. Whatever it is that you've experienced or still experiencing is a part of your progress. The Bible says, "And we know that all things work together for good to those who love God, to those who are the called according to His purpose" (Romans 8:23). The good, the bad and the ugly have all been strategically positioned for your greatness. So, see it all as your learning period!

As you begin to rebuild your life, no matter what life throws at you, stand tall and believe in yourself. The world is filled with lies and negativity. But don't pay attention to them. Once you start paying attention to the world's lies and negativity, it torments you for the rest of your life. The period of challenges is a learning phase, which will pass, sooner or later. The question is, will you come out a better version of yourself or still remain the same old person? Don't let a fall along the road be the end of your journey. Focus on the end result.

Start by declaring your commitment. Write it out. I (insert name), declare and make a commitment to myself to rebuild my life.   Forgive yourself for the things you have done that hold you back from living your truth. Starting today, I will forgive myself for:

- being hard on myself

- not letting my voice out sooner

- trying to live up to societal and others' expectations

- undermining my own abilities

(What do you forgive yourself for? Insert _____ _____) Recognize the things you have done and will be doing.   I am proud of myself for:

- taking little steps to work towards rebuilding my life

- taking risks out of my comfort zone to break away from the expectations

- following my heart even though it is scary

- finding the strength to speak my mind and think about limitless possibilities

(What are you proud of yourself for? Insert __ _____)   State your commitment to yourself.   I am committed to:

- letting go of what is behind me

- being kind and loving myself unconditionally

- owning up to who I am and what I am

- not betraying myself to satisfy others

(What are you committed to yourself? Insert _____ include your signature.

Here are steps you can take (if you're not already taking them) to become a better version of yourself:

- Embrace God's promises and His unconditional love for you.

- Thank Him for having brought you this far.

- Believe and have confidence in yourself.

- Never settle for less.

- Think! Think!! Think!!!

- Take that step you need to take without fear - learn that business, master that skill, go back to school, if need be.

- Surround yourself with positive=minded people.

- Don't be afraid to fail. Failing doesn't make you a failure; it's another great chance to start again. If Plan A fails, try Plan B, if B fails, try the next. Don't ever give up on yourself!

- Most importantly, have faith in God!

Your life is yours to live. It is up to you to make it the life of your dreams. So, if you have the opportunity to make a change that will lead to your greater happiness, grab it with both hands. Be the change you want to see in you!

# NINE

## THE FOCAL POINT

*"Now faith is the substance of things hoped for, the evidence of things not seen. For by it the elders obtained a good testimony." (Hebrews 11:1-2)*

—————— ◦◦◦◦◦ ——————

Permit me to ask you this very important question: On what are you anchoring the ship of your voyage to greatness? What gives you the confidence that you will be able to fulfill all the requirements that we have discussed so far – having the right frame of mind, discovering and following your passion, discerning good and bad friends, making wise use of your time, recovering your losses and making progress in all areas of your life? Is it by merely depending on your natural intelligence and determination? Well, it doesn't really work that way.

To start with, you may find it extremely challenging

taking some of the steps outlined so far in your own strength. On the other hand, you may even, by an extraordinary amount of determination, keep to all the pieces of advice given earlier, and still find yourself feeling frustrated, rather than being fulfilled. How so? Here is the answer: "I returned and saw under the sun that—The race is not to the swift, Nor the battle to the strong, Nor bread to the wise, Nor riches to men of understanding, Nor favor to men of skill; But time and chance happen to them all." (Ecclesiastes 9:11),

Now, the question is, who is in control of "time and chance"? It is God Almighty. This is why faith in God and His promises is pivotal to your success in life. It is the core component of greatness that makes every other component easy for you and also work in your favor.

## FAITH AND ITS SIGNIFICANCE

We just cannot do without faith, because there is a deep vacuum in our lives that is especially reserved to be filled by faith in God. Besides, as humans, there are several limitations we have and impossibilities we encounter that only the power of God can help us overcome. Specifically, on our journey to greatness, we need faith in God for:

1. **Discovery of purpose and destiny.** Greatness begins with knowing why you were created in the first place and what your mission is in the world. What's the easiest way to discover this purpose? Of course, it's through your faith in God. This is what prompts God to reveal things you do not know about your purpose, past, present and future life to you. He says, "Call to Me, and I will answer you, and show you great and mighty things, which you do not know." (Jeremiah 33:3).

2. **Favor and connection to destiny-helpers.** It is one thing to know your purpose but it is quite another to get the favor and strategic positioning you need to put your potentials to maximum use and march your way to the top. Only faith in God can obtain divine favor for you and make your divinely-appointed helpers to locate you. One day of favor from God is better than ten years of labor. This is what faith can do in your life.

3. **Uncommon inspiration and ideas.** Signals of powerful inspirations and world-changing ideas are always being transmitted from heaven. However, only those whose hearts are attuned to God by faith can catch these signals. Consider Joseph and his interpretation of Pharaoh's dreams. No other person could

catch the signals of the interpretation, except Joseph whom God specifically revealed it to and his life was transformed from that moment. This can happen to you too by faith in God. You could be the solution that everyone is waiting for in your community, church or organization.

4. **Protection from destiny-killers.** There have been many talented people who ended their careers and sometimes their lives in shame, disgrace and calamity. The reason? They fell into the snares of Satan and the destiny-killers he had prepared for them. How can you detect these destiny-killers and their deadly traps? It is through faith in God. The Bible says, "For whatsoever is born of God overcometh the world: and this is the victory that overcometh the world, even our faith." (1 John 5:4, KJV).

## NURTURING YOUR FAITH

Now that you know the power and possibilities of faith in God, the next question is, how does one develop such faith that works wonders? Frankly, effective faith isn't something sudden; it must be exercised to grow. Do you remember Peter in the Bible? He was just a mere man, just like you and me. Was he perfect? No! He made a whole lot of mistakes in his faith journey but ultimately received strength. In his epistle (2 Peter 1:3-11), he gives us a set of guidelines on building up our faith:

1. **Have a good relationship with God.** God gives us all that we need for life and godliness through the knowledge of Him. How much do you know God? You can develop a relationship with God by making Christ the Savior and Lord of your life. Thereafter, spend constant time in prayer, studying of God's word, praising God and fellowshipping with other believers. Recognize that faith isn't measured by anything else but the quality of your relationship with God. Make building a close relationship with God your top priority in life, and know that God will respond by giving you more and more faith.

2. **Believe even when you don't see answers to your prayers.** Remember that God is always at work, but sometimes He's working behind the scenes until the right time to reveal His answers to your prayers. Believe in who Jesus really is and in what He has done for you. Recall God's promises from Scripture. Ask God to give you the confidence to continue to listen to His guidance and act on it.

3. **Be attentive.** I mentioned something about "heavenly signals" earlier. Amidst the hustle-

bustle of daily living, learn to pay attention to God. Be sensitive to the nudging and promptings of the Holy Spirit. He will always guide, instruct and correct you.

4. **Remember God's promises.** Understand that, while you may be unfaithful to God, God will always be faithful to you. Read God's promises in the Bible and know that you can count on them. Persevere in tough circumstances, trusting that God will deliver on His promises to you.

5. **Grow in the fruit of the Spirit.** Peter counsels us to add to our faith, virtue; and to virtue, knowledge; and to knowledge, temperance; and to temperance, patience; and to patience, godliness; and to godliness, brotherly kindness; and to brotherly kindness, charity. Take careful note of all these qualities and try as much as possible to live in them daily.

6. **Don't sacrifice obedience on the altar of common sense.** Understand that    faith's security lies in obedience. Rather than basing your decisions on circumstances you can seek wisdom from God, who has the benefit of a complete perspective on every situation. Rely on God's guidance instead of your own limited understanding.

7. **Sincere assessment.** You can always ask any of your honest friends to assess your Christian life, so as to be able to work on areas in which you are lagging behind.

8. **Avoid temptation.** Make the right choice always and flee from all appearances of evil. Resist the devil, whichever way he comes, and he will flee from you.

9. **Live in consciousness of God and heaven.** It is one thing to say that you have faith but it's a different thing to show it. How have generations of successful believers been able to overcome life's challenges? It is by trusting God and setting their affections on heavenly things (Colossians 3:1-2).

Why do people give up their faith or hope? It is because they stop focusing on their heavenly goals and shift their entire gaze to the things of the world, such as earthly goals, dreams, material items or experiences. Don't get me wrong, all these things aren't wrong to have, but the problem arises when we seem to make them more important to God and they become our small gods.

## APPLYING FAITH TO LIFE'S CHALLENGES

When the storms of life blow upon you, how do you react? Do you stay calm, trusting in

God's abiding presence, or do you allow fear to overpower you? Oh yes, I had been a victim of such times myself. There had been times that I cried and got worried; there had been times that I was down; but eventually, I learned to hand all my worries completely over to the One who is more than capable. And He has never failed me.

With God, your biggest setbacks can become your biggest comebacks. With God, you can move from being a victim to being a victor. With God, you can sail through the deepest and darkest valleys of life and walk high on the mountain. It's important to not let your obstacles in life tear you away from your faith. Instead, these are the moments when you need faith the most. If you are stuck in a pit of despair, don't give up. Reach out and call God's name. He is there right beside you.

I urge you to learn to relinquish the desire to control everything in your life. No matter how big your problem may feel, or how impossible it may seem for it to get better, know that nothing is too difficult for God to handle. Jeremiah 32:27 states "I am the Lord, the God of all mankind. Is anything too hard for me?" When faced with an enormous obstacle, don't focus on how big the problem is. Focus on how strong God's power is. He is much more powerful than any obstacle you will ever face! This helps to shift your perspective and gain the confidence needed to know you can handle it with God's help. God will help you knock down that wall in front of you.

Hand over the steering wheel of your life to God and never try to figure anything out. Simply believe in God's omnipotence and let your faith work for you!

# TEN

## YES, YOU CAN!

*"…the people who know their God shall be strong, and carry out great exploits."(Daniel 11:32)*

---

I believe that, so far, you have been mightily inspired and loaded with the catalysts of greatness that are beginning to manifest in you already. Let me conclude by saying that we all aspire to do, become and have great things, but many of us haven't created the life we want. I want you to know, very importantly, that this is YOUR life. The way you live it depends on you alone. It's a choice you alone can make, a step you alone can take.

Are you living a life of purpose or a life of complaints? Everyone wants to be great in life. But for you to achieve this, you need to believe in God, yourself and your God-given abilities.

Let me remind you:

- You can become whatever you want to be.

- You can have a successful life.

- You can do anything through the strength of God.

- You can be the difference and also make a difference.

- You can radiate positivity.

- You can be the best.

- You can achieve greatness.

- You can attain greater heights.

- You can be happy.

- You can be at peace with yourself.

- You can inspire and motivate millions of people.

Yes...YOU CAN! The challenges you face in life are all stepping-stones to your greatness. The good, the bad, the ugly are all strategically positioned for your greatness. Greatness needs challenges, Olivier Poirier – Leroy said: "My goal + hard work = I win!"

What really happens, THE SETBACKS, THE

FAILURES, THE FRICTION, THE GRIND. The moments that tests you, that will push you to the brink of giving up.

But please, make no mistake; you need these moments of strife. Why? Because they are precisely what will separate you from the rest who crave the exact same thing.

I often try to picture what I want and where I want to be in 10 years' time. Have you ever thought of this for a second? Five years from now where do you want to be? Remember, this is your life and your cross. You should make a plan of how you want to spend or live it. This is your responsibility, and no one else's. Believe in yourself and know within yourself that you are capable. Have you ever seen a glory without a story? NO!

I use the following illustration most times I find myself in a challenging situation:

When you want to bake a cake, what do you need?

- The ingredients (flour, eggs, yeast, baking powder, sugar, spices, salt, milk, oil, flavors and other add-ins.)

- Preheat the oven and grease the cake pan (STEP 1).

- Cream the butter and sugar (STEP 2).

- Add eggs and flavors (STEP 3).

- Stir together the flour and baking powder and salt (STEP 4).

- Pour the mixture into the pan and bake (STEP 5).

- After 1 hour 15 minutes, the cake is ready, right? (STEP 6)

- Add icing and decorations (STEP 7).

Note: STEPS 1, 2, 3, 4, 5 are the main processes during the preparation. It was mixed with every effort and care, with adequate portions. It looked messy and stressful. That's the main work in the preparation. A process has to be followed to achieve the desired result. That is exactly how our life is.

In STEP 6, it was placed in an oven right? What does an oven feel like? Ouch! Yet, the heat and the hotness of the oven make the baking perfect. The oven represents the fears, tears, sleepless nights, worries, depression, pain and problems we go through while we are being shaped for greatness.

The cake is baked and ready! How does the cake look at this point? Smells nice, looks nice, beautiful and fresh. This is exactly what we become after overcoming all trials and challenges.

The final step involved the cake being iced, shapened, designed and decorated. How did the cake come out? Better, more beautiful, more attractive. The cake didn't melt away with all the mixtures and battering and the heat. The cake came out perfect and strong. The same is also applicable to our lives.

Did you also notice that some parts of it were scraped off to give it a befitting look. While passing through those challenges, God is working in you, Romans 8:18: "For I reckon that the suffering of this present time shall not be compared with the glory which shall be revealed in us." The befitting look represents God's glory radiating in our lives. This is exactly how we become after every challenge. It's not forever, it's just for a while and it will pass away. Challenges make us strong in God. The greater your destiny, the greater your challenges, remember the cake went through different processes before reaching its final step.

## RECAP: STEPS TO GREATNESS

- Be prayerful.
- Know God and trust His word concerning your challenges.
- See the big picture (Walk by faith and not by sight).

- Pay attention to that still small voice of the Holy Spirit.

- Get rid of habits that draw you back.

- Distance yourself from negative people.

- While the challenges are still there, plan on how to overcome them.

- Avoid distractions.

- Never stop learning (Learn every day!)

- Focus and be committed.

- Be disciplined.

- Keep few friends that inspire and motivate you.

- Take responsibility; after all, it is YOUR life.

- Believe in yourself and your vision.

- Don't ever give up on God and don't give up on yourself.

- Make positive declarations in faith every day.

- Listen more, talk less.

- Having a mentor is a great idea.

- Take some time out alone, enjoy the fresh air. This helps you to think more, relax more and re-strategize.

Now, you are all set for dominion. Your next level life is here. Take your place among champions — that's certainly where you belong!

# ABOUT THE AUTHOR

Ope Adebayo is a young, brave, ambitious, and highly intelligent lady. A Christian, who loves God and has been a great inspiration to many. She has a bachelor's degree in Economics and currently working on her master's in Managements.

Ope is a creative entrepreneur and author of Greatness is in You. She is a good singer and a lover of music. She enjoys reading and writing. Over the years she found herself increasingly obsessed with the people's stories as she undertakes a journey to helping people discover the greatness in them.

She is married to her best friend, Adewale and are blessed with a handsome boy, David. Together they live in Houston Texas, USA.